FIND YOUR
Y

Answers to Life's
Most Important Question

HigherLife Development Services, Inc.
PO Box 623307
Oviedo, FL 32762
(407) 563-4806
www.ahigherlife.com

Find Your Y - Answers to Life's Most Important Questions
© 2023 by André Butler Ministries. All rights reserved.

Printed in the United States of America
10 9 8 7 6 5 4 3 2 1

PB ISBN: 978-1-958211-80-9
EPUB ISBN: 978-1-958211-71-7

ENDORSEMENTS

"Pastor Andre is being used mightily by God in our genera-tion to bring creative insights and understanding to the people of God. "Find your Y" will help you discover the powerful secrets of God and revolutionize the way that you think!"

Tim Timberlake
Lead Pastor of Christian Faith Center
Author of 'Abandon'

"Grab a cup of coffee and your notebook as Pastor André leads you into the journey of discovering your Y. Discovering why you exist and uncovering your purpose is one of the most important undertakings you can embark on. In this book, Pas-tor André leads the reader on a personal journey in discovering their purpose, leaving them with practical steps that will enable them to live their Y for the entirety of their lives. I highly recommend that you read this book, live this book, and share it with loved ones so you all can live your Y."

Pastor Kerrick Butler, lead pastor
Faith Christian Center, Austell, Georgia
fccga.com

"One of the most asked questions and most important questions by and to Christians today has to do with our purpose in life. Find your Y by Pastor André answers the question in a way that we all can understand no matter our age, background, or socioeconomic status. He writes in a manner which captivates and connects us to the message that God through him is proclaiming about our purpose. Someone once said that the purpose of a thing is established by its creator. You were created by God for a specific purpose in this life. Find out today by reading this new book — Find your Y."

Pastor Stanley Scott II
Faith Family Church, Houston, Texas

"Have you ever asked these questions? "Why am I here? What is my purpose in life? What was I created to do?" Anyone who is serious about living life as God intended has asked these questions at one time or another. My friend, Pastor Andre' Butler will take you on a journey to discovering the most important truth to your existence. When you know why you exist and commit to following God's plan and purpose for your life. Everything you need to find fulfillment will begin to fall in place. Listen to every word in this book and watch it change your life!"

Dr. John Barton, Founding Pastor
Living Life Church, Lafayette, LA

ACKNOWLEDGEMENTS

I would like to first give honor to my Lord and Savior, Jesus Christ, who has saved me and given me the honor of helping Him save the world. Also, to my church family Faith Xperience Church, my parents Bishop Keith Butler, Pastor Deborah Butler, Pastors Lee & Michelle Ferguson & Ministers Joel & Kristina Jenkins. Without all of you, I would not be who I am. I also would like to acknowledge Rev. Kenneth W. Hagin, Kenneth and Gloria Copeland, and the many other outstanding men and women
of God who taught me God's love and his ways. I am forever grateful!

TABLE OF CONTENTS

INTRODUCTION

"The two most important days of your life are the day you were born and the day you figure out why."

MARK TWAIN

Are you living life frustrated and unhappy? Is it getting harder and harder for you to get up and go to work? Are you not as successful as you had hoped to be? If so, you are not alone. There is an epidemic of frustration, discontent, and low productivity in the world. I am confident that a major reason for all this discontent is that people have not found their "Y" in life, their purpose. The goal of this book is to help you find your Y and live in it fully so that you are the happy, productive, and prosperous person God wants you to be.

This book is going to take you on a journey. I am going to walk with you as God talks to you. God will talk to you about why you are here on this Earth, what you are supposed to do with your life, and what your next steps should be. Even if you feel like you know your Y and you are living in it, God will reveal to you more about your purpose and how to flourish in it.

I personally believe this is one of the most important books I have ever written. This book will change your life. God wants you, I want you, and the world needs you to fully live the life that God has planned for you from the moment that he first thought about you. It's time to find your Y!

CHAPTER
1

THE IMPORTANCE
OF FINDING
YOUR Y

Someone once said that a career is what you are *paid* for, but a calling is what you are made for. That's a fact. We all entered this world under different circumstances. Maybe you were conceived by a man and a woman who were married and in love, or perhaps you were born into a single-parent home. Maybe you came into this world due to a tragedy, such as rape. No matter what the circumstances were around your arrival, God brought you here for a reason.

God brought you to the Earth to do something specific for Him. When God created this planet, everything had a purpose. He created the stars, the trees, and the seas for a purpose. Even those little ants in your house that annoy you have a purpose.

Think about it—even in our world today, everything is purpose-driven. A glass's purpose is to hold liquid, right? A napkin's purpose is to wipe up messes. A pen's purpose is to write. A car's purpose is to transport you. Everything God created has a unique purpose, and you are no different. When we talk about your Y, we're talking about your unique calling, your unique purpose—what God sent you to the Earth to accomplish. The goal of this book, Yxist, is to help you find your Y so that you can enjoy the productive and prosperous life that God wants you to have.

Dr. Victor Eagan and his wife, Catherine, wrote a book called *How to Discover Your Purpose in 10 Days*. In it, they explain that you will never be completely satisfied or fulfilled until you are walking in God's plan for your life.

The Eagans outline the real and practical benefits of knowing and living in your Y. You will:

- Lead a full and satisfied life.

- Feel good about yourself.

- Feel as though your life really makes a difference.

- Be content.

- Enjoy your job and career.

- Have a more stable marriage.

- Waste less time and energy on unproductive activities.

- Feel greater fulfillment and purpose in your life.

- Feel a level of personal satisfaction and increased confidence.

- Stop feeling like you're wandering endlessly through life.

- Take control of your life and make your dreams a reality.

- Unlock and fulfill the greatness within you.

Put simply, there is an abundance of good that happens when you find your Y.

Dr. Myles Munroe, a Bahamian evangelist, famously said, "The wealthiest place in the world is not the gold mines of South America or the oil fields of Iraq or Iran. It is not the diamond mines of South Africa or the banks of the world. The wealthiest place on the planet is just down the road. It is the cemetery. There lie buried companies that were never started, inventions that were never made, best-selling books that were never written, and masterpieces that were never painted. In the cemetery is buried the greatest treasure of un-

> # IN THE CEMETERY IS BURIED THE GREATEST TREASURE OF UNTAPPED POTENTIAL.

tapped potential."

Isn't that true? The graveyard is full of unfulfilled purpose. And that is what happens when people don't discover and live in their Y. In fact, when we don't know or fulfill our purpose, it can lead to many problems, like these:

- Depression
- Lack of self-appreciation and respect
- Low self-esteem
- Premature death or aging
- Lazy or lackadaisical attitude
- Inability to be successful

- Underachievement
- Financial instability

As you can see, it's a huge problem when you don't know your Y or if you're not living in your Y.

GOD CREATED YOU WITH PURPOSE

Look at Jeremiah, for example. God created him with a purpose in mind:

> *"God said to him, 'I knew you before I formed you in your mother's womb. Before you were born I set you apart and appointed you as my prophet to the nations'" (Jer. 1:5, NLT).*

God saw a need in the nations, and He made and sent Jeremiah to fulfill that purpose. I want you to really take in what I just said: *He saw a need, and he created someone to fulfill that need.*

I am writing a screenplay. One day, as I was sitting in Starbucks waiting for my kids to finish a class, I started creating characters. I already had a good idea of who my main character would be, and as I typed the description of the character into my iPad, I knew I created that guy for a reason. My book needed that character, and he would serve an important purpose in my story.

That's what God did. He looked at the world and said, "I need a prophet." He then made Jeremiah to be his mouthpiece, a megaphone to the nations.

This isn't just true of Jeremiah; this is true of you, of me, of everyone. God created you with a purpose. God saw a need on this Earth, and He created you to meet that need. You have a divine destiny. Please repeat what I said: "I have a divine destiny." God didn't wait until you were born to figure out your Y. He sent you to this Earth with an intention, a purpose. Don't you think it behooves you to figure out what it is?

YOUR Y IMPACTS NOT JUST YOU, BUT ALSO THOSE AROUND YOU

When you find your Y, it not only impacts you; it impacts the world around you. It impacts the world your family lives in. It impacts others who follow your example. Most importantly, it impacts the people God has called you to reach for Him. God needs you to find and fulfill the purpose He has for you.

You were born with the ability to change a life. There's somebody you are supposed to help save by simply being in your Y. There is somebody who hasn't heard about Jesus or doesn't understand all that God has done for him or her. When you find and fulfill your Y, you will give *them* a chance to follow Jesus.

Take Samson, for example. He had a Y before he was even born, before his mother was even pregnant. The people of Israel had become, in essence, slaves of the Philistines. Their land was occupied and had been so for forty years. The Scripture says:

> *"The angel of the Lord appeared to Manoah's wife and said, 'Even though you have been unable to have children, you will soon become pregnant and give birth to a son... You will become pregnant and give birth to a son, and his hair must never be*

cut. For he will be dedicated to God as a Nazirite from birth. He will begin to rescue Israel from the Philistines" (Judg. 13:3, 5 NLT, emphasis mine).

Samson's Y was to launch the deliverance of his people from the Philistines. Although he made some major mistakes before he left this world, he did, in fact, launch their deliverance from the Philistines.

ACKNOWLEDGE THAT YOU ARE HERE FOR A REASON

If you start looking through the Bible, you will find that almost every man or woman of God had a stated

> **I EXIST TO HELP PEOPLE EXPERIENCE THE FUTURE GOD HAS FOR THEM.**

life mission. They figured it out at different times and at different ages, but they all had a life mission from God.

I discovered my life mission a number of years ago. It became evident to me that I exist to help people experience the future God has for them. That's my life mission. What's yours? What has God revealed to you about the life mission He has chosen for you? Can you write it down? Can you state it? Many people can't. Yet it's vital that every one of us figures it out.

Life just doesn't work when you don't know your Y or are not living in it. A number of years ago, I found myself in a very different place. I knew my Y, but I wasn't really "in it." I was used to being someone who, for the most part, had been living in my purpose in God's place, in God's time. I was used to that. I always had a certain level of fulfillment and prosperity. But in that particular season, it was like my heart had been ripped out. I felt like there was a hole in the middle of me. I had never been as unhappy as I was at that time in my life.

I knew what the problem was. Some things were out of my control, but I knew that I wasn't *in my purpose*. I wasn't doing what God had called me to do, and I was miserable. You would not have wanted to be around me. I ended up regularly going to God in prayer just to build myself back up, day after day. I was building myself back up just to survive, to keep myself from destroying my marriage or my relationship with my kids.

Those are the kinds of things that happen when you aren't in your Y. You are doing a disservice not only to yourself and God, but also to those around you. Unfortunately, that is how many people are living. They can't serve others well because they are just trying to survive, to get from one day to the next. You will never be completely satisfied until you live out God's Y for your life.

You are here for a reason. Say it to yourself: "I am here for a reason." What is that reason? What is your life mission? What is your Y? It matters. Whether or not you figure it out matters to God, to your family, and, most of all, to you.

In Genesis chapter 12, God told Abram that He

wanted him to leave everything and go to an unfamiliar land:

> *"Now the LORD had said unto Abram, get thee out of thy country, and from thy kindred, and from thy father's house, unto a land that I will shew thee" (Gen. 12:1, KJV).*

Abram was probably seventy years old at the time. So if you think it's too late for you to find your Y, it isn't. Abram did not follow God's direction immediately; it took about five years for him to go to the land God told him about. That land was key; it was where he would accomplish his Y. Notice what God says to him next:

> *"I will make you into a great nation. I will bless you and make you famous, and you will be a blessing to others. I will bless those who bless you and curse those who treat you with contempt. All the families on Earth will be blessed through you" (Gen. 12:2–3, NLT).*

Here, God is telling Abram his life mission. He tells him, "I will make you into a great nation...All the families on Earth will be blessed through you." Abram's life mission was to become Father Abraham. Through him would come the great nation of Israel and, ultimately, the Savior of the world, Jesus. (This is partly why God changed Abram's name to Abraham, which means "father of many nations.")

FIND THE TREASURE AT YOUR Y

Many of us are familiar with a treasure hunt and the idea that you are looking for the X on the map. X marks the spot. If you can get to the X, underneath that X is going to be a treasure.

Well, I'm here to tell you, Y is what marks the spot in our lives. If you can get to your Y, you'll find treasure. You'll find that God will prosper you. You'll find that God will cause you to be fulfilled. You'll find that God will use your life to help others. You'll find that your life will be everything that you and God wanted it to be.

Do you see why it's so important that you find your Y? Because Y marks the spot. That's where you'll be fulfilled, you'll do great things, and God will do great things for you. If you don't know your Y, or if you are living in a Y for which you were not created, you will feel awkward and unfulfilled. But when you get in the Y God has for you, you will soar. You will enjoy greatness because in your Y is blessing and fulfillment.

END-OF-CHAPTER
REFLECTIONS

As you begin searching within yourself and God to lead you to your Y, keep these things in mind:

- Before God formed you, He knew you. He has a purpose designed specifically for you.

- If you live your life with unfulfilled purpose, it can produce devastating results for you, those around you, and those God created you to reach for Him.

- You will be blessed, fulfilled, and productive if you live in the Y God has intended for you.

CHAPTER
2

YOU ARE HERE
FOR A REASON

We said it earlier, but I want you to say it again: "I am here for a reason." Yes, in fact, you are here for a reason. And when you figure out what that reason is—what your Y is—you will strike gold!

In Acts, God talks to Paul about his Y. At first, Paul was going in the opposite direction of what God planned for him. He was persecuting God's people. Then God appeared to him on the Road to Damascus. Here is what the Scripture says:

> *"Now get to your feet! For I have appeared to you to appoint you as my servant and witness...Yes, I am sending you to the Gentiles to open their eyes, so they may turn from darkness to light and from the power of Satan to God. Then they will receive forgiveness for their sins and be given a place among God's people" (Acts 26:16-18 NLT).*

When I was growing up, my mother would always wake me up in the morning by turning the light on. I hated it! I'd try to keep my eyes closed no matter what because I wanted to keep sleeping. But every morning, my mom would turn that light on, and that would be my indication that it was time for me to wake up and start moving.

Paul's mission was to preach the Good News about Jesus to people who did not have a covenant with God (the Gentiles). By preaching the Gospel, Paul was shining its light on their hearts. God's hope was that once they were exposed to the light, they would open their

> **AT FIRST, PAUL WAS GOING IN THE OPPOSITE DIRECTION OF WHAT GOD PLANNED FOR HIM.**

spiritual eyes and turn from Satan (darkness) to Him (light). Turning the Gentiles toward God was Paul's Y. He was driven by his Y. The only way for you to be driven by your Y is if you know it and embrace it.

Just like God appeared to Paul on the Road to Damascus to reveal to him his Y, God is ready to speak to you about your Y. He did not put you on this planet for a purpose and then decide to hide it from you. He is not playing hide and seek with you. In fact, I wouldn't be surprised if He has already been talking to you at different moments in your life about your purpose.

YOU NEVER KNOW WHEN OR WHERE HE WILL CALL YOU

I had no interest in being a pastor when I was a kid. It's funny. I was having a conversation with two of my kids, and I told them, "It's time you figured out your Y." My eight-year-old is the queen of questions, but my eleven-year-old is blunt, like her mother. She said to me, "Well, I just hope God doesn't call on me to be a pastor because I don't want to be a pastor." My eight-year-old agreed and said, "Yeah, me neither. I don't want to be a pastor, either." I explained to them that I didn't want to be one, either, but then I found out that it was what God called me to do. Now I can't imagine doing anything else.

I grew up in a church called Word of Faith, where my dad was the pastor. I thought my dad's job was the most boring job in the world and wanted nothing to do with it. I felt just like my kids do.

When my daughter was in kindergarten, someone asked her to write down what I do. I still have her answer on my desk. She wrote, "My dad preaches two times a

GOD WAS CALLING ME TO THE MINISTRY.

day and shakes people's hands." That is how I felt about my dad when I was young. I thought he just preached and dealt with crazy folks. Preachers' kids can tell you some interesting stories. About 90 percent of what I saw was great, but the 10 percent that wasn't great always stood out. I thought on more than one occasion, "No, I don't want anything to do with that."

One day when I was seventeen, everything changed.

Meadowlark Lemon from the Harlem Globetrotters came to preach at Word of Faith. I was an athlete, so of course, a basketball player really caught my attention. After he spoke, I went home and listened to a recording of his talk. And when I did, God spoke to me. One of the words that stood out was "evangelism." I didn't know what that was. I went and asked my parents, "What is evangelism?" At first, I thought God was telling me to be an evangelist. But once my parents explained what it was, I recognized that God was talking to me about my purpose. I knew in my heart that God was calling me to the ministry.

At that time, I had just received a full scholarship to the University of Michigan. I decided to take the scholarship, thinking I could get into ministry later. That is our family business, after all. I figured I could wait, and my dad would teach me when I was ready.

I went to my orientation at the University of Michigan and had my classes lined up. The next month, I was at youth camp, and God was really moving in a service. Youth camp was always amazing like that. We would take a few days, give God time, and He would always show up. My cousin and I were on our knees at the altar, praising God, and He spoke to both of us right there on the spot. He said, "I want you to go to Rhema Bible Training Center." I recognized that God wanted me to go to ministry school, but I still had the full scholarship and didn't want to lose it. I still planned to go to the University of Michigan and decided that once I graduated, I would go to Rhema.

However, I remained open to God's direction. A few weeks later, as I was pacing around a hotel room praying, I asked Him, "*When* do you want me to go to Rhema?" Suddenly, it was like somebody was in the room! I had heard preachers say that, but it was the first time I experienced it. I heard, *"Now."* I knew what that meant. I had to leave my scholarship behind and make my way to Rhema.

Once I made the decision, things started working out well. It turns out Rhema had a basketball team, and they wanted to give me a scholarship to play there. At the time, I wasn't thinking about the ministry I would build *after* Rhema. But, at the end of my second year, it became apparent to me that God wanted me to go home to be a minister—right then.

So that is what I did. I came back home to be a staff minister, and after a year, the Lord started talking to my dad about opening a church in Arizona. He asked me to preach at his new church in Phoenix on Wednesday nights. I said to my dad, "I'm here to serve."

I was twenty-one years old, single, and wasn't thrilled about flying to Arizona every week. But I went. The first Sunday came, and my dad said, "You're preaching." The second Sunday came: "You're preaching." The third Sunday, and then the fourth…you get the idea. Three years later and with the help of my spiritual parents who nudged me to do what was in my heart, it was finally solidified in my heart that a major part of my life mission was to be a pastor.

I'm convinced that just as God was able to reveal to the Apostle Paul and a skinny teenager from Detroit our Y, He is able and willing to do the same for you.

GOD WANTS US TO KNOW OURSELVES

God wants you to know yourself. We have all heard the well-known phrase that was inscribed on stone by ancient philosophers, statesmen, and law-givers at the entry of the temple of Apollo: "Know thyself." What the writers didn't understand was that the profound truth in this statement didn't come from their intellect, but from the true and living God. Yes, God really does want you to know yourself. And one of the things that will help you understand yourself is to discover how God wired you, how He built you.

I want to help you to understand how God wired you so that you can understand your Y.

"Just as our bodies have many parts and each part has a special function, so it is with Christ's body. We are many parts of one body, and we all belong to each other. In his grace, God has given us different gifts for doing certain things well" (Rom. 12:4–6 NLT).

Notice that he says that we all have *different gifts*. The word "gifts" here means spiritual endowment or miraculous faculty and is translated as talents in the Am-

> **YOU HAVE AN ABILITY THAT SUPERSEDES NATURAL ABILITY.**

plified Bible. You have an ability that supersedes natural ability. You have a God-given gift to do something very well. I like to call it a *grace gift*—a supernatural talent that God gave you for your own fulfillment and for changing the world. Using this gift is easy for you. You're motivated toward it and passionate about it. You see things through the lens of it, you love it, and you are energized by it.

In a sense, you have your own superpower. Everyone knows Superman's powers; he can run fast and fly, among other things. We could spend all day talking about different superheroes like him who each have their own special abilities. Well, each of us also has our own abilities, and together, we make up God's superhero team on Earth.

God has given you a special ability. If you can find out what that specific ability is, it will help you discover what your Y is. Look at a fish, for example. You can look at its gills, and even if you don't know what it is, you could conclude that it has the special ability to swim in water. If you see a bird, you might not know much about it, but you can look at the wings and conclude that it has the special ability to fly. Everything in this world is designed to fulfill its purpose, and you are no different. God intentionally made you with this ability. How you're made points to what you're supposed to do.

I want you to discover the gift that's given to you. So in the next chapter, we are going to explore your design.

END-OF-CHAPTER
REFLECTIONS

God sent us to this world with a purpose. As you reflect on what your purpose is, keep these facts in mind:

- God is ready to share your Y with you; He does not want to hide your purpose from you.

- Your purpose may be exposed to you when you least expect it. Be sure you always have your eyes and heart open to receiving what God is telling you.

- Working diligently to know yourself can lead you to discover your Y.

CHAPTER
3

THE Y TEST

The *Y test* is something we can use to grasp how God has wired us, and it can point us to the Y he has for each of us.

In this chapter, I will ask you several questions that will help you identify your personality type, what you're passionate about, your talents, and your dreams. Keep in mind that answering these questions alone will not reveal your Y, but you may discover it at the intersection of your answers.

There is no need to panic; this is nothing like the tests you had in school! I am simply asking you to evaluate yourself and to let God speak to you as you do so.

WHAT IS YOUR PERSONALITY TYPE?

Determining your personality type can give you clues about what your Y is. Although I am not going to spend much time on this, I encourage you to take a short test at gifttest.org and/or take a free DISC test online to identify your personality type.

> **DETERMINING YOUR PERSONALITY TYPE CAN GIVE YOU CLUES ABOUT WHAT YOUR Y IS.**

WHAT IS YOUR PASSION?

"But thanks be to God, who planted the same earnest zeal and care for you in the heart of Titus" (2 Corin. 8:16, AMP).

God planted in Titus a zeal and care for the people of Corinth. Notice that this was not a natural thing. God did it, So it was a supernatural thing. Because God put it in him, it was natural for him to have this zeal and care, this passion for people.

What are you passionate about? If you aren't sure, here are a few questions for you to explore:

- What do you enjoy doing most?

- What do you enjoy learning about?

- What have you felt fully alive doing?

- What would you do if money were not an issue?

When was the last time you were firing with all cylinders? Think about a time when you wanted to stop the clock and ask, "Can I just keep doing this all day?" Let's say you inherited $10 million. Would you be doing the job you're doing right now? If the answer is no, then why are you in that job? Take a moment to reflect on the last time you were in a state in which you were having a great time and felt like you were doing something that mattered. That is a clue that can point you to your Y.

WHAT IS YOUR TALENT?

Next, let's identify your talent. I am fascinated at how much the Scripture in Exodus reveals about how God gives us talents to help us fulfill our purpose in the world. In this Scripture, Moses is talking about the building of the tabernacle:

> *"And Moses said to the Israelites, 'See, the Lord called by name Bezalel the son Uri, the son of Hur, of the tribe of Judah; And he has filled him with the Spirit of God, with ability and wisdom, with intelligence and understanding and with knowledge and all craftsmanship, to devise artistic designs, to work in gold, silver and bronze, in cutting of stones for setting, and in carving of wood, for work in every skilled craft'" (Ex. 35:30–33, NLT).*

God gave Bezalel special abilities. He was good at these things—so much so that others could recognize them, and God could use him to help build His tabernacle.

What are you good at? Ask yourself:

- What work am I proud of?
- What have people acknowledged, recognized, or rewarded me for?

• What is my God-given talent?

If you are having trouble with this, ask yourself what your friends and family members would say you are good at. Or ask them directly, "What do you think I am good at?" They can give you godly counsel. And if someone close to you says you are bad at something, you should listen.

WHAT IS YOUR GRACE GIFT?

Your *grace gift* is a supernatural talent that God gave you for your own fulfillment and for changing the world. Using this gift is easy for you, you're motivated toward it, passionate about it, see things through the lens of it, you love it and are energized by it.

> *"In his grace, God has given us different gifts for doing certain things well. So if God has given you the ability to prophesy, speak out with as much faith as God has given you. If your gift is serving others, serve them well. If you are a teacher, teach well. If your gift is to encourage others, be*

encouraging. If it is giving, give generously. If
God has given you leadership ability, take the
responsibility seriously. And if you have a gift for
showing kindness to others, do it gladly" (Romans
12:6-8 NLT).

Listed in these Scriptures are seven gifts found in the Body of Christ. Those gifts are:

- Prophecy (called the gift of Speaking in 1 Peter 4:10–11)

- Serving

- Teaching

- Encouraging

- Giving

- Leadership

- Kindness (or Mercy as it is called in the King James Version)

Notice that Paul writes this as though each individual has primarily one of these gifts (although we may have some of the other gifts as attributes, we have a special ability to operate in one of them). He also noted that we should not only know our gift but that we should use our gift.

Be careful to not confuse these gifts with the Gifts of the Spirit found in 1 Corinthians 12. Careful study of the Bible reveals that those gifts work differently than these. For example, we cannot turn the gifts of the Spirit on or off as is being commanded here. Only God can do that.

Paul recognized and mentioned his grace gift in 1 Corinthians 3:

> *"According to the grace of God which is given unto me, as a wise master builder, I have laid the foundation, and another buildeth thereon. But let every man take heed how he buildeth thereupon" (1 Cor. 3:10, KJV).*

What Paul is saying in this Scripture is that God gave him grace, ultimately, to start churches that would set people free and help build God's kingdom. Paul didn't earn this power; it's something he received

PAUL DIDN'T EARN THIS POWER; IT'S SOMETHING HE RECEIVED FROM GOD.

from God, and it was natural for him to use it to glorify the Kingdom of God.

I've seen this with my father, Bishop Keith Butler. It's just natural for him to start churches. People ask him how he does it, and he almost can't explain it because it is a God-given grace.

I traveled with him when I was in my early twenties. He would preach in Michigan at 6:30, 7:00, and 8:45 in the morning and then travel down to Atlanta and preach at noon. Then he would fly to Phoenix for a 6:00 service in the evening. He did that every week for about a year. When I traveled with him, I would be wiped out, but it would seem like he was getting stronger. When God gives you grace, you are empowered with a supernatural ability to do something. You will be powerful when you are working in your Y. God's power will cause you to prosper in what you put your hand to do; it will cause you to have success.

Take Joseph, for example. His grace gift was clearly leadership. He was so successful in the workplace that his heathen boss eventually concluded that the Lord was helping him. Even in prison, Joseph's abilities brought him success. Ultimately, his gift helped him become second in charge in a country that was not his own at the young age of thirty.

"The Lord was with Joseph, so he succeeded in everything he did as he served in the home of his Egyptian master. Potiphar noticed this and realized that the Lord was with Joseph, giving him success in everything he did...From the day Joseph was put in charge of his master's household and property, the Lord began to bless Potiphar's household for Joseph's sake. All his household affairs ran smoothly, and his crops and livestock flourished. So Potiphar gave Joseph complete

administrative responsibility over everything he owned…. Before long, the warden put Joseph in charge of all the other prisoners and over everything that happened in the prison. The Lord was with him and caused everything he did to succeed" (Gen. 39:2–3,5, 22–23 NLT).

God's grace is the X factor, or the "it" factor. Without it you can't accomplish much of anything—surely nothing of eternal value. With God's grace, anything is possible!

A number of ministries offer tests that can help you identify your grace gift. (Unfortunately, a number of them confuse ministry gifts, the gifts of the Spirit, and the grace gifts, so be aware of that when using one.) However, notice that Paul didn't use one. He expected God's people to be able to look at the list and identify themselves.

An example that may help is if someone drops a plate of food at a church event, you could get the following responses:

- Prophecy: "God told me that was going to happen."

- Serving: Immediately starts picking it up.

- Teaching: "The plate is supposed to be balanced with food, etc."

- Encouraging: "That's okay, you'll do better next time!"

- Giving: "Have my plate."

- Leadership: Starts giving orders so it's cleaned up.

- Kindness: "Are you okay?"

Which of these gifts best describes you?

WHAT IS YOUR DREAM?

In the book of Genesis, Joseph had a dream:

"One night Joseph had a dream, and when he told his brothers about it, they hated him more than ever. 'Listen to this dream,' he said. 'We were out

in the field, tying up bundles of grain. Suddenly my bundle stood up and your bundles all gathered around and bowed low before mine!' Soon Joseph had another dream, and again he told his brothers about it. 'Listen, I have had another dream,' he said. 'The sun, moon, and eleven stars bowed low before me!' But while his brothers were jealous of Joseph, his father wondered what the dreams meant" (Gen. 37:5–7, 9, 11, NLT).

God placed a dream in Joseph's heart, and his brothers hated him for it. Now, most people know that if you dream a dream in which everybody is bowing to you, you should keep it to yourself. But Joseph was so excited about the dream that God gave him that he couldn't keep his mouth shut. Think about it—if you tell your kids you're going to take them to Disneyland next week, they will talk about it all week, to everyone around them. They're excited! Joseph was so excited about his dream that he couldn't stop talking about it.

God gives us dreams as well. He might or might not give them to you while you're sleeping, like he did Jo-

> # GOD PLACES HIS DREAM FOR OUR LIVES IN OUR HEARTS.

seph. But God places His dream for our lives in our hearts.

When identifying your dream, ask yourself these questions:

- What is it that I can't shut up about?

- What do I daydream about?

- What keeps me up at night in excitement?

- What do I hope I will have accomplished at the end of my life?

END-OF-CHAPTER
REFLECTIONS

God wants you to know yourself. I want to challenge you to get a piece of paper out and start answering the questions presented in this chapter. Start evaluating where you are in life, what you're doing, and why you're doing it. Ask yourself if you are in the right Y. As you answer these questions, you will figure out how God has wired you.

CHAPTER
4

WHAT HAS GOD
TOLD YOU?

We've been looking at how God wired you with the expectation that doing so will clue you into the Y God created you for. However, there is one major question that you must get the answer to that will help you discover what God sent you to this world to accomplish. You see, you can't find your Y on your own. Maybe you've tried. Maybe that's why you have a college de-

YOU CAN'T FIND
YOUR Y ON YOUR OWN

gree in one field but work in another, or you just keep switching from one job to the next, to the next, looking for fulfillment.

There is a main ingredient that you must have, and without this ingredient, you will wander and wander, never finding your purpose. But when you add this ingredient to your life, you can quickly gain clarity. So what is this special ingredient that we need to discover our Y? The answer is God. Without God, you not be able to find your Y. When you add God to your journey, when you allow Him to pour His wisdom into you, you will begin to understand why you are here.

The good news is that God is eager to give us His wisdom for our lives:

"If any of you lack wisdom, let him ask of God, that giveth to all men liberally, and upbraideth not; and it shall be given him" (James 1:5, KJV).

"If you don't know what you're doing, pray to the Father. He loves to help. You'll get his help, and won't be condescended to when you ask for it" (James 1:5, MSG).

God is clearly in the business of speaking to people. People sometimes struggle with this concept. They don't believe that God speaks to us. But of course He does. If man can make cell phones that we can speak to and that respond to our voices, can't God do the same thing with people? The Bible tells us that God is ready to speak to us. He is prepared to give you the wisdom you need when facing any situation in your life. That includes if you're not sure what your Y is or what the next steps in your Y should be.

God won't criticize you or hold back from you the wisdom you need. No, He's waiting for you to ask for it. The dinner bell has rung. He is saying, "Come and get it!"

God sends life-changing gifts from heaven into your life when you simply ask Him. God is not in heaven trying to hold you back from you what He created you for. It's quite the opposite—He has been waiting for you to come to Him and spend enough time with Him to discover the gifts He has for you.

COMMUNICATE WITH GOD USING THREE TYPES OF PRAYER

You might be wondering, "How do I go to God and ask Him what my purpose is?" The answer is prayer. Prayer is the way we communicate with God. In the book of Matthew, we are told how simple it is to pray to God:

> *"Ask, and it shall be given you; seek, and ye shall find; knock, and it shall be opened unto you. For every one that asketh receiveth; and he that seeketh findeth; and to him that knocketh it shall be opened. If ye then, being evil, know how to give good gifts unto your children, how much more shall your Father which is in heaven give good things to them that ask him?"* (Matt. 7:7–8, 11, KJV)

In the Scripture above, three types of prayer are mentioned:

1. **The asking prayer**—This is commonly called "the prayer of faith." It's the type of prayer you say when you believe that God will give the thing you've requested the moment you complete your prayer. You pray this prayer one time and then thank God for the answer until it arrives.

2. **The knocking prayer**—Commonly called "the prayer of supplication," this heartfelt, earnest

prayer is called striving, laboring, and more in the Scripture. It's often what people refer to when talking about "praying through" or spiritual warfare in prayer.

3. **The seeking prayer**—Receiving the answer to this type of prayer can take time. It's not that God isn't giving wisdom immediately. It's often that it takes time for us to be in a position to receive and recognize the wisdom that God has for us. If you spend time in God's presence seeking wisdom, you will eventually receive your answer.

It is often the seeking type of prayer that you will use to find your Y. God's promise to you is simple: If you will seek Him, he will make your Y clear to you.

SEEK HIM WITH ALL YOUR HEART

In the book of Jeremiah, God shows us that seeking is not something done just by the mind:

"And ye shall seek me, and find me, when ye shall

search for me with all your heart" (*Jer. 29:13, KJV*).

Seeking is done with your heart. It's not mechanical. When you are truly seeking something, you are en-

---

SEEKING IS DONE WITH

YOUR HEART.

---

gaged, both mentally and emotionally. You are focused. Finding what you're seeking is a priority.

My wife and I had tickets to a Lecrae concert. He is a Christian hip hop artist, and we were really excited about seeing him perform. But the day before the concert, we couldn't find the tickets. We had the babysitter lined up, we had spent the money on the tickets, and now we couldn't find them. So my wife and I got the kids, and we all started looking for the tickets. We were moving furniture around and communicating with each other. And thank God! We found them!

When something is really important to you, you will seek diligently for it! What if you lost $1,000? You would stop whatever you were doing to find it! And that's what has to happen when you are discovering your Y. You need to have the type of mentality that compels you to take extraordinary measures to find it. Finding your Y needs to be a priority.

Kenneth Copeland, president of Kenneth Copeland Ministries, a worldwide organization that has ministered to millions, says there have been times in his ministry when he would need to go away to a cabin or hotel for a few days just to hear from God. He'd do it to escape from the distractions of the busy world around him and focus on God. I can relate to that.

Yet that's a hard thing to do, to just disappear for two or three days to pray. Most of us can't do that, but what you can do is make seeking God about your Y a priority in your life. It could be the main thing you are focused on in prayer for a season until you receive the answer that you're seeking. I like to call that making it your "prayer project." If you make discovering your Y your prayer project, it can lead to you hearing from God and having Him do something great in your life. If you're going to find your Y, you must make prayer a priority.

GOD HAS ANSWERS GOOGLE CAN'T GIVE YOU

God knows your Y, and you need to seek Him to find out what it is. I have been using the term "seek," but you can also say you are "searching" for your Y.

We all use Google to search for information. Sometimes searching can take time. Maybe you need to find someone to do some work at your house, or maybe you need a better understanding of something going on in your workplace. So you'll go to Google, and you'll spend some time searching for the knowledge you want.

> **GOD HAS ANSWERS GOOGLE CAN'T GIVE YOU.**

God has answers Google can't give you. And if you learn to seek God—if you put the same type of effort into that as you would into gaining information for other purposes—you will get information that's vital to discovering your Y, or learning the next steps in your Y.

When you are seeking God, it is important to spend time thanking God, praising Him, and worshiping Him with all your heart first. This will help ensure that you are in tune spiritually with Him and able to recognize when He is speaking to you.

Even when you pray in the Spirit, or speak in tongues, you can get to a point where you do it by habit, without much thought. But praying should not be something you are doing like it's just a religious duty; your heart needs to be engaged. God's will is very clear that when we need to hear from Him, we ought to search with all our hearts.

God has been trying to get your attention. It's time that you do what it takes for the ears of your heart to be tuned in to heaven.

HOW GOD SPEAKS TO US

That begs the question, "How will God speak to me?" In the Bible, there are a number of ways that God speaks to his people. God is a Spirit, and He made us spirit beings as well. We're more than bodies and more than minds. We are spirits, and God communicates with us spirit to spirit. This is similar to how my phone can send a text message to your phone. God's messages to us come in one of three forms:

1. **The Bible**—The Bible is the number one way that God speaks to people. Just like a CEO might dictate a memo to an administrative assistant to speak to his or her employees, God dictated His words to His followers to deliver them to us. Thus, any other method that God uses to speak to us about our particular lives will not contradict what God has already written to us in the Bible.

2. **The Inward Witness**—Have you ever seen a snow globe with a toy character inside? The Holy Spir-

it lives in your spirit in much the same way, and He witnesses to your spirit when you are on the right track—and when you're not. Some individuals refer to these leadings as a velvety peace feeling or a check in your heart, meaning a feeling that something just isn't right. (Kenneth Hagin used to say checks feel like taking a shower with your socks on!) Another way of looking at these leadings is to think of them as green lights and red lights. When you have a green light in your heart, you're on the right track, and when you have a red light, you're not. I like to call these moments "nudges" in your heart. These are moments when it's like the Holy Spirit is giving you a gentle elbow in your heart to guide you in the right direction. Here are a few examples of this in Scripture:

"And when Silas and Timotheus were come from Macedonia, Paul was pressed in the spirit" (Acts 18:5).

"God's Spirit touches our spirits and confirms who

we really are" (Rom. 8:16).

3. **The Inward Voice** – At times, God speaks to us from inside our hearts in a still, small voice. This is not a voice that you hear with your physical ears but with the ears of your heart. I like to call this "the whispers of God."

The majority of the time that God speaks to us, it's through these three methods: the Bible, whispers, and nudges. There are a few other methods worth mentioning, too.

4. **The Voice of the Holy Spirit**—In addition, the Holy Spirit might speak up in your heart in a more forceful voice. Once again, you don't hear this with your natural ears. But in this case, it can be so forceful that you might think you did.

When God made it clear to me that He wanted me to forgo a full scholarship to the University of Michigan to go to an unaccredited Bible school in Oklahoma called Rhema, it was by the voice of the Holy Spirit. It was so "loud" that, for a second, I wondered if someone was in the room. God sometimes does this when there is rough sailing ahead. You will need to have had this experience with Him as an anchor to help you stay on board with his plan.

5. **Visions and Dreams**—Like He did with Joseph, Jesus's stepfather, and Paul on the Road to Damascus, God speaks to people through visions and/or dreams. If you have a vision or dream, remember that if what was said does not agree with what the Bible teaches, the vision or dream did not come from God. Also, the Bible says to "prove all things," so be sure to seek godly counsel from a pastor or some other form of spiritual leadership to ensure that you have heard from God.

At times, God will send someone to "prophesy" to you about your life, including your Y. He has done that with me from time to time.

For example, one part of my Y involves writing screenplays. One Saturday afternoon, I reached a point where I was so frustrated with the lack of progress in that area of my life that I told God, "I quit." I didn't need to write screenplays (I was already a pastor), and I wasn't going to anymore. The next day, we had a guest speaker at my church. A minister friend of mine came to hear the speaker and then came to the back of the church after the service to meet them.

After we all socialized for a while, and when it was time to leave, she stopped me and said, "God told me to tell you that you are not to stop writing screenplays." She went on to give me further instruction from God. I'm sure that my jaw hit the ground! I hadn't even told my wife yet that I had quit, and here was this woman of God giving me a message that she couldn't have known

THAT'S HOW GOD USES PROPHECY—AS A TOOL TO CONFIRM WHAT YOU AL-READY HAVE IN YOUR HEART.

I needed. Needless to say, God was using her to speak to me so that I would continue to do what God created me to do.

I already knew I shouldn't quit writing screenplays, and this confirmed it. That's how God uses prophecy—as a tool to confirm what you already have in your heart. If it's new information that's being "prophesied" to you, then ignore it, but if it confirms what God has already put in your heart, it might be God speaking to you.

Sometimes the way that God reveals your Y to you throughout your life is similar to peeling back the layers of an onion. He won't reveal it all at one time. If He told you everything up front, you probably wouldn't even start. It would be overwhelming, so He just gives you just the amount of information you can handle at one time.

When you find him, God will speak to you about your Y in one of these ways.

LOOK FOR THE SUPERNATURAL, NOT THE SPECTACULAR

Perhaps as you read this book, you are realizing that He has already been speaking to you about your Y. I guarantee you that He has. Sometimes the problem is that we've been looking for the wrong thing.

I'll share something that happened to me recently. For easily a year, I prayed about something that was on my heart. It was something very, very important to me. I was starting to get frustrated because I couldn't nail down what God was saying—or so I thought. I kept praying about this thing, and finally, it started affecting many different areas of my life because I felt like I was in limbo. I'm accustomed to feeling like I know exactly what God is saying to me. But this time was different. So I started asking in prayer, "God, why aren't You talking to me about this?"

I know what the Bible says about seeking and finding God's direction, and I was trying to figure out what I was doing wrong. Finally, one day while I was in prayer, God made clear to me that I was barking up the wrong tree. I was missing it in two ways. Number one, I had already made up my mind about what I wanted, and I was looking for God to agree with me vs. hearing what *He* had to say about it. Number two, I was looking for God to lead me in a spectacular way instead of in a *supernatural* way.

If you asked me during that time what was happening, I would have said I was waiting to hear the voice of God, and it needed to be strong enough that I knew it was God. But as it turns out, the whole time, He was nudging me in my heart, and I wasn't paying attention to it. I kept ignoring it, overriding it, because I wanted God to speak to me in a stronger, more spectacular way. Finally, I sat back and evaluated what had been in my spirit. And boom! It was sitting there all along. I wasted months, maybe a year, trying to get God to tell me something He had already told me.

A friend of mine had a similar experience. He had a big question in his mind, and he had been seeking the answer for years. It was affecting the direction of his life. Even after God used me and other men of God to talk to him about it, he was still struggling to recognize God's direction. Eventually, he followed the simple nudge that had been in his heart all along, and boom! God blessed him with the desire of his heart.

We have been talking about finding your Y and looking to God to guide you in it. But you can't forget how He leads. You don't get to tell Him what method He gets to use to guide you. You have to walk with God to hear His voice. You have to spend quality time with Him daily so that you are spiritually sharp. Once you find this spiritual sharpness, you will begin to notice that you are getting little nudges and whispers in your heart.

I want to encourage you as we continue to go on this journey together to stop looking for a trumpet to sound, indicating the direction that God wants you to go. Instead, look in your heart for God's whispers and nudges.

God has been talking to you about your Y. He's been trying to get your attention. It's time that you do what it takes for the ears of your heart to be tuned in to heaven.

END-OF-CHAPTER
REFLECTIONS

- The main ingredient you need when seeking your Y is God. He will lead you to, and guide you on, your journey.

- Prayer is communication with God. Make finding your Y your prayer project.

- Be engaged in prayer; don't just do it out of religious duty.

- The main ways that God speaks to us is through the Bible and through whispers and nudges in our hearts.

WHO MOVED MY Y?

I recently attended my twenty-year high school reunion. It was a lot of fun seeing people I hadn't seen since graduation. I have seen some of my classmates since we graduated, but sitting there talking, many of us agreed that back then, we had no idea where we would be, or what we would be doing, twenty years after graduation. I know I didn't.

When you hear some people's stories, you are amazed at the turns their lives have taken. When you face these turns in life, you want to make sure they are God-led turns. You want God to be the one who gives you direction. And when God gives you new direction, you need to make sure you follow it.

You see, sometimes we can get to a place where we do understand who we are and what God has called us

GOD'S PLAN FOR OUR LIVES HAS STAGES.

to do, yet we fail to recognize that God's plan for our lives has stages. You might be in one stage of your Y, and God is trying to get your attention to move you on to the next stage.

The Apostle Paul's Y had stages. At one stage, he was teaching in a local church. In the next stage, he started churches. In the following stage, he was to testify about Jesus before kings. In his last stage, he wrote many of the letters that we call "epistles" in the Bible. If you read Paul's life story, one of the things that stands out is that he always seemed to recognize when it was time to move on to the next stage. This understanding came as a result of his continuing to seek God and stay open to hearing His voice. And you need to do the same.

This requires that you do these three things:

1. Develop the habit of spending time with God every day.

2. Stay sensitive to God's direction.

3. Keep seeking God to make sure you are still following His plan.

In the Old Testament, there was a time when the people of Israel lived in the wilderness and literally saw God's glory cloud on a regular basis. They learned that when the cloud settled in one place, they were to settle there as well, for as long as the cloud did. But when the cloud moved, they were to pack up the camp and move with it.

I've often heard that some ministers never get out of the first stage of their ministry. That means they heard from God, and they were walking in what God told them to do, but when God shifted, they kept walking on the same path they had been on before. The cloud had moved, but they didn't move with it. So eventually, they hit a wall. They get frustrated that they're not seeing success. Sometimes they die early, and they miss out on everything God wanted to do for them because when God shifted, they missed it.

Sometimes when this happens—when life doesn't seem to be going in the right direction—people blame everybody else. They might even look down on others who are having success. When that happens, it's time to go back to that heavenly search engine and find out what God is saying.

If things are going wrong—if you've been sitting in a dry spot for a while—then at the very least, you need to go to God and ask Him what's going on. He might tell you to stay the course and tell you that you're doing fine. Or He might tell you that He tried to tell you last month, or even last year, to change your direction, but you didn't listen. Sometimes that's what happens with churches, ministries, and businesses—they keep following the same path, and eventually things dry up. That's because they didn't continue to follow God's direction. Make sure that's not you.

SEEK GOD'S GUIDANCE EVERY STEP OF THE WAY

In 1 Samuel, David finds himself in a terrible situation. He has a misstep. God had called him to defend Israel against the Philistines, but instead, he joined with the Philistines and tried to fight against Israel. When he got back home, he found that his home has been attacked. The enemy's army had come in, destroyed the town, and taken their wives and kids.

Of course, all of David's men were upset. They were angry with David and even talked about stoning him. David was understandably depressed, but he didn't let

DAVID ASKED GOD FOR HIS DIRECTION.

himself stay there. He gots in God's presence and allowed Him to build him up. Then David asked God for His direction.

"And David said to Abiathar the priest, Ahimelech's son, I pray thee, bring me hither the ephod. And Abiathar brought thither the ephod to David. And David enquired at the LORD, saying, 'Shall I pursue after this troop? Shall I overtake them?' And he answered him, 'Pursue:

for thou shalt surely overtake them, and without
fail recover all'" (1 Sam. 30:7–8, KJV).

David sought God's direction, ultimately saying, "Shall I chase after this troop that destroyed my home?" God answered him, saying that he should. I find it interesting that David didn't automatically react when he discovered the devastation and begin pursuing his enemy immediately. Instead, He realized that he needed to hear from God. In this case, he got a quick answer, which was critical because if he was going to catch the troops, he needed to get moving. So he went after them and recovered everybody and everything that had been taken.

God directed him every step of the way. Later, when David became king, the Philistines came to attack. But David didn't run right to the battlefield. He went back to God and asked what he should do. God told him he should go to the battle, so he did, and he was victorious. The Philistines returned again to the same battlefield, but David didn't just follow the last plan God gave him. He went back to God for new direction, and God alerted him of the enemies' plan to ambush him. David followed the new battle plan that God gave him and was victorious, again. David knew that God's direction might be different in even similar situations.

If God tells you to do something, don't assume that means you should do it that way the rest of your life. Sometimes God will give you new direction, and if you follow that direction, you will have even greater success than you have in the past.

CHANGE DIRECTIONS TO AVOID GETTING STUCK IN A RUT

It is critical that we, as God's children, watch out for the disease of "pride." We must not allow our egos to determine the direction of our lives. Some of us have to let go of the ego, not the Eggo! If God hasn't been able to do anything significant through you for the past five or ten years, something is wrong.

If you were to read the entire Bible one time, you wouldn't put it down and say, "Well, I'm done with that book." No! There is always a fresh revelation in the Bible. You need to continue to pick up the Bible and at-

> **THERE IS ALWAYS A FRESH REVELATION IN THE BIBLE.**

tentively study it throughout your life because there's so much in it that will change you, help you grow spiritually, and equip you to save your world. That is the mentality you must have when it comes to living in your Y. God wants you to get better, wiser, and more productive.

You often hear about the problem of being stuck in a rut in the business world. That's why companies like Blockbuster are no longer around. They had a great business model and were doing well, but then the culture shifted. They didn't begin offering their services and products online. The people at the top might have been saying, "We don't need to do that; we're Blockbuster!" Well, the guy who made that decision is the "broke buster" now. You can't live your life like that.

You have to go from good to great and change when change is needed.

God often does things in seasons. When He begins to deal with you about moving into the next stage of your Y, *go with it.* Trust that God knows best and that change is needed. Follow God's plan *all* your life, and your life will be as great and fulfilling as you have always dreamed.

END-OF-CHAPTER
REFLECTIONS

- One of the things that will help you on this journey to your Y is keeping a prayer journal and documenting what God says to you when you pray to Him. Keep it in front of you. It will help you follow God's plan and fulfill your Y.

- Pray continuously for God's direction; guidance He gave you in the past might no longer be appropriate for your life situation.

LIVE YOUR LIFE IN YOUR Y

By this time, I hope you have really begun to zone in on your own personal Y. Now I want to talk to you about *applying* it.

> *"God has given each of you a gift from his great variety of spiritual gifts. Use them well to serve one another" (1 Pet. 4:10, NLT).*

Someone once said, "The anointing of God makes you better than your ability, smarter than your IQ, and more charismatic than your personality. The anointing is the it factor and the X factor. Without it, you can't accomplish much of eternal value. With it, all things are possible!" You have that anointing! You have the God-given ability to carry out your Y, and God wants you to use it!

One of my favorite movies growing up was *Superman 2*. Superman had decided to try to live life as a normal man and purposely lost his powers. Then disaster struck, and everyone was looking for Superman to save them. They needed him to use the gifts he was born with to save the world. The same thing is true about you.

Your family needs you to use your gift. Your church needs you to. Your neighbor needs you to. Your neighborhood needs you to. Your colleagues need you to. The world needs you to. Using your God-given gift in your Y is why God sent you here. He looked into this world and saw a hole that only you can fill. And that hole will not be filled until you apply your Y.

Let's look at four keys to applying your Y.

1. TAKE THE LEAP

"Genesis says, 'Now the LORD had said unto Abram, get thee out of thy country, and from thy kindred, and from thy father's house, unto a land that I will shew thee. And I will make of thee a great nation, and I will bless thee, and make thy name great; and thou shalt be a blessing: And I will bless them that bless thee, and curse him that curseth thee: and in thee shall all families of the earth be blessed'" (Gen. 12:1–3, KJV).

God was asking Abram to take a giant leap of faith. Can you imagine if God showed up to you this afternoon and said, "I want you to leave the United States of America. I want you to leave your family and your friends. I want you to leave your parents, even though they might be a little older now." Even in this day and age where you can pick up the phone or Skype with someone anywhere in the world, you would struggle with that, especially if He said all that and then told you that when you get to the airport, only then will He tell you your destination.

Yet that is exactly what God required of Abram. Why? Because God needed him to live his life in his Y. And the same thing is true for you.

Unfortunately, Abram didn't obey God immediately. God said He wanted Abram to leave and go to the land. Abram left his home, but he went to Haran, which was only halfway. He left his country, but he didn't go to the land God told him to go to. God also instructed him to leave his kindred. Well, Abram didn't leave his kindred, either; instead, he took his nephew, Lot, with him. Last,

God told him to leave his father's house, but Abram took his father with him as well. And as long as Abram lived in Haran instead of his Y, he was not qualified to receive what God had promised him.

God has promised you a great future. But you can't experience that while living in your Haran. Haran for you might be staying at a job or in a career God didn't send you to, dating a person God didn't send to you, or living a lifestyle God is not fully pleased with.

Sometimes in our lives, we want to go only halfway. We don't want to take a leap of faith. We want God to bless us in Haran. But it doesn't work like that. Like Dr. Martin Luther King once said, "Lightning makes no sound until it strikes." At some point, you have to take the leap of faith and just obey God. You must step into your Y and trust that God knows you best and will take care of you.

2. BE Y-DRIVEN

In John 4, Jesus arrived to a well around lunchtime, and His disciples went to go get some food for Him. While He was sitting there, a woman approached Him. Ultimately, after talking to her, He succeeded in leading her to believe Him. She ran to go tell others what she learned about Jesus.

> *"In the meanwhile his disciples prayed him saying master, eat. But he said to them, 'I have meat to eat that you know not of.' Therefore said the disciples one to another, 'has any man brought him ought to eat?' Jesus saith unto them, 'My meat is to do the will of him that sent me, and to finish his work.'"* (John 4:31–34, KJV).

Jesus said to them: "My meat is to do the will, the desire of him that sent me and to finish his work." In other words, "I've had my fill. I've already gotten what fulfills me. What fulfills me is doing what God sent me to do. That's what satisfies me. That's what drives me."

I think that it's very interesting that Jesus used the

term "meat" because it implies hunger. You eat because you're hungry—at least that's how it's supposed to be, right? He was telling them what to be hungry for—for doing what God sent them to do, for completing their Y. And then He said, "My meat is to finish His work." In other words, "I'm going to keep on eating. I'm going to keep doing the work that He wants me to do. This is what I'm focused on."

Then in verses 35–38, He tells them that they ought to be the same as Him, that they ought to be looking in the fields of the world and seeing that people are ready to be saved and fulfilled by bringing them into God's family. He was telling them that they ought to hunger for fulfilling what God put them on this Earth to do as. I like to call this "being Y-driven."

Like Jesus, you must to be Y-driven. You must not only understand what God put you on Earth to do but also have a hunger for fulfilling that and a willingness to do whatever it takes to carry that out. Many of us know what it's like to be cupcake-driven. A pregnant woman knows what it's like to have cravings interrupt her night (and so does her husband!). Well, God wants us to be Y-driven.

One individual said this: "There's one quality that one must possess to win, and this is definiteness of purpose, the knowledge of what one wants, and a burning desire to possess it." Zig Ziglar said, "Outstanding people have one thing in common: an absolute sense of mission."

Jesus had a sense of mission. Paul had a sense of mission. He was constantly writing and saying, "I'm here to minister to the Gentiles. This is what Jesus told me on the road to Damascus. This is what I'm chasing after." That's what he was about. You've got to learn to live your life by your Y. You need to think like Jesus and Paul: "If I'm here for this purpose, then this is what I'm focused on. This is what I'm chasing after. This is what excites me."

Paul would say things like, "What's our joy? What's our hope? What is it that we rejoice about? It's about the fact that you, the Gentiles, will be standing before Jesus one day." He was possessed with that that craving to fulfill that long-term goal. What are you possessed with? You ought to be possessed with fulfilling the Y, the purpose God has for you.

One way to help you find your Y is to keep your life uncluttered. Rick Warren said, "It's impossible to do everything people want you to do. You have just enough time to do God's will. Purpose-driven living leads to a simpler lifestyle and a saner schedule."

Once you discover your Y, you need to craft your life around it. Recently, I've been coming across more and more articles about how unproductive multitasking is. You just don't get things done as quickly or as well as you would if you just focused on one thing at a time. Sometimes as Christians, we multitask too much. We've got to find out what our purpose is and pursue that. When we're good at that, we need to be comfortable in the fact that we are doing what we are here to do.

John the Baptist was someone who accepted that he was simply here to pave the way for the Messiah. He recognized that, and he was so good at it that Jesus said there was no greater prophet than him under the Old Covenant.

Here in Detroit, we had a basketball player by the name of Ben Wallace who played for the Pistons. He couldn't shoot that well, and he couldn't dribble that well. But what Ben Wallace *could* do was play defense, which includes rebounding. He became the best rebounder and defensive player he could be, and he helped lead our Pistons to a championship. Sometimes you've got to stop trying to be Michael Jordan and just be Ben Wallace. As long as you have a championship ring on your finger, who cares what your role was?

Once you've discovered your Y, you must be driven by it. Craft your life around it. Be great at it. Whatever you do for God, be great at it. That happens when you're driven by your Y.

Watch out for distractions! Most of us have heard the statement that "People who lose their way lose their Y." This was definitely true of Samson and David; they got in trouble because they got their focus off their Y. Samson was not thinking about delivering Israel; he was thinking about Delilah, and it cost him his life. David was not on the battlefield helping the Israelites in battle; he was pacing the rooftop, bored. He ended up with Bathsheba, and it wrecked his family.

Make sure you don't get distracted. Focus on your Y. You might have to ask yourself the question, "What's distracting me from my Y?" Look at that, and make some changes so that you are actually Y-driven.

3. DON'T GIVE UP

It's easy to have a romanticized view of things happening easily once you take your leap of faith and become Y-driven, but that isn't always how things work. You have an enemy who does not want you to do what God has called you to do. Satan will try anything and everything to stop you from having a positive impact on the lives of others. I believe that is what happened to Abram.

Remember, God had promised Abram that when he got to the land, he would be blessed with a great nation, which meant a son. When Abram finally got to the land, a number of the things that God promised him happened relatively quickly. But after thirteen years, he still didn't have a son. So he gave up on God's plan and decided to follow his own. That created great problems in his home and the world we live in today.

You can't give up on your Y just because things aren't happening as quickly as you would like. If you are where God told you to be, even if things haven't happened yet, don't try to make it happen your own way. If you do, it will do nothing but cause problems.

At the end of those thirteen years, God appeared to Abram and told him that his wife, Sarah, would give birth to his son. But she was almost ninety years old and had been barren for her entire life. When Abraham heard that, he laughed at God.

"The Scripture reads, 'Then Abraham fell upon his face, and laughed, and said in his heart, "Shall a child be born unto him that is an hundred years old? And shall Sarah, that is ninety years old, bear?"' (Gen. 17:17, KJV)

God appeared and said the same thing He had told

him twenty-four years earlier—and Abram laughed at him. Abram believed God enough to leave his old life behind twenty-four years earlier, but now he was in such disbelief that he was actually laughing in God's face. How did this happen? He had given up on his Y. He now viewed what God had promised as impossible. Abram fell out of the arena of faith and entered the arena of disbelief. If you are not careful, you can find yourself there, too.

When God says something to you and you believe it, but then after some time it still hasn't happened, it can be disappointing. It can be easy to stop believing that God will do what He promised.

Just imagine that you have been hearing all about your purpose, and that when you get to your Y, God will do this, and God will do that. You sit, and you wait, but it has been a while, and nothing is happening. God is still showing you this dream, this vision, but at that point, you might be tempted to think, "God, how are you going to do that? That's not even possible." Of course you would. The enemy will make sure to tempt you in this way. But the moment that you yield to that temptation, you will have given up.

You can't give up. When you step out of faith, you are guaranteed to fail. What is there to lose by continuing to believe? If you choose not to believe, you get nothing. If you choose to believe, God will do what He said. That's what happened with Abram. God helped him to believe again, and then God came through like He said He would.

SPEAK WHAT GOD SAYS TO YOU

One of the things that God did that helped Abram believe again was change his name. God told him that his new name was Abraham, which meant "father of a great multitude." This, coupled with God putting in front of his eyes a constant reminder of His promise, led Abraham to the place that Romans 4 talks about:

"Who against hope believed in hope, that he might become the father of many nations, according to that which was spoken, so shall thy seed be. And

being not weak in faith, he considered not his own body now dead, when he was about an hundred years old, neither yet the deadness of Sarah's womb: He staggered not at the promise of God through unbelief; but was strong in faith, giving glory to God" (Rom. 4:18–20, KJV).

Maybe you are in this situation. God may have said that XYZ is going to happen with your business, your family, or your finances. He has given you His word about what is going to happen in a specific area of your life. You need to speak that word every day as well.

In my life, I believe that God has spoken to me about pastoring a church of one hundred thousand people. That's a lot of people, I know! Nobody has a church that large in America. But we are getting close. I believe that my church will get there, and I am speaking that as truth every day.

When you decide to speak what God says to you, and look at His promises, every day, it will help you to not stagger or weaken your resolve. It will help you to give

God glory for it happening ahead of time, even though you might not see results or the answer to your prayer just yet.

DON'T LET YOUR X BLOCK YOUR Y

You are the only barrier that can stop God from doing what He wants to do in your life. God's plan for your life is bigger than everything that is coming against it. Don't allow temptation or disappointment to cause you to step away from your Y. We call these feelings your "X." Don't let that happen.

You've really got to watch out for your X because it will block your Y. For more clarification, let's look to Mark, which says this:

"And these are they by the wayside, where the word is sown; but when they have heard, Satan cometh immediately, and taketh away the word that was sown in their hearts" (Mark 4:15, KJV).

Don't allow yourself to become hard-hearted toward

God because of what you see happening in your life at that moment. That's an X that will block your Y.

> *"The seed on the rocky soil represents those who hear the message and immediately receive it with joy. But since they don't have deep roots, they don't last long. They fall away as soon as they have problems or are persecuted for believing God's word" (Mark 4:16, NLT).*

What do you do when trouble comes your way? Or you encounter people who attack you? Don't allow offense to rise in your heart against God or against people. That's an X that will block your Y. Sometimes you have to forgive the same people over and over and over again.

There is one area of my life in which the enemy will try to get to me through a particular thought. That happened to me recently. Somebody texted me early on a Saturday morning. I don't know why anyone would text that early on a Saturday, but I love the person, so I read it. It wasn't anything bad, but it reminded me of something bad that had happened to me. And that something tried to stick with me all day. For a while there, I had a hard time with it because it made me angry. But I finally got to a place where I made the choice to move on. I was not about to let the enemy trick me into blocking my Y.

That's what happened with Joseph. His family had put him in a bad situation, and he was angry. He made a mistake, although not a very big one. Running off at the mouth at the age of seventeen isn't that unusual. Regardless, his brothers threw him into slavery. So there he was, in a horrible situation, but he decided to be faithful. He continued to do his work for the Lord, regardless of his situation, and God was able to prosper him in it.

Do not give up on your Y. Don't use what's happening in your life as an excuse to go back into the sin that God delivered you from.

4. COMPLETE YOUR Y

In football, a pass is not completed until a receiver "completes the process" of the catch. It doesn't matter how great the catch may have seemed to be on replay; if the player did not complete the process, it's an incomplete pass. The same is true concerning your purpose. It's not good enough to start living in your Y; you must *complete* it! You must finish the job.

> *"In 2 Timothy, Paul said this at the end of his life: 'I have fought a good fight, I have finished my course, I have kept the faith'" (2 Tim. 4:7).*

Paul revealed that his mission was accomplished. He knew why God had sent him, and he ran after it. He didn't give up, even though he was thrown in prison, beaten, and whipped. He finished. And that is what God wants for you—He wants you to finish living out your Y.

I have seen people who have done well for years but then begin a downward spiral out of their Y. I've heard stories of ministers like this. God used them for decades, but when they got to the end of their lives, they got caught up in illegal or immoral activities. They got distracted, or pride got in the way; they began to think they were too smart for anybody to teach them anything. So they don't complete the process. They didn't complete their Y.

God wants you to produce more and more goodness in this world until He returns. He wants you to get to the place where you can say, "I finished my course." At the end of your life, you want to be able to sit back and say, "I completed my Y. I finished my course. I'm ready to go home." You want to walk into heaven, stand before the King, and hear Him say to you, "Well done, my good and faithful servant. I made you ruler over a little bit, and now I'll make you ruler over much. Enter into the joy of the Lord!"

END-OF-CHAPTER
REFLECTIONS

- Live according to the purpose God has for you. And watch what God does with your life.

- Be vigilant, and refuse to let the enemy, Satan, distract you from completing your Y.

ABOUT THE AUTHOR

With an undeniable passion for equipping others to experience the future God has for them, André Butler is on a mission to share God's desire to prosper His people in every area of their lives, and His command for them to do their part in winning the world to Jesus. The Pastor of Faith Xperience Church (FX Church) in the heart of Detroit, he is a sought-after conference speaker and host known for his practical and relatable approach to preaching God's word. He also is a Screen-writer and Movie Producer and serves as the President of Faith Xperience Films and the Faith X Network. A graduate of Rhema Bible Training Center, Pastor An-dré also holds a bachelor's degree in Management from Kennesaw State University. He resides in Metro Detroit.

Pastor André Butler

André Butler Ministries
PO Box 43627
Detroit, MI 48243
info@myfaithx.com

IF YOU'RE A FAN OF THIS BOOK, WILL YOU HELP ME SPREAD THE WORD?

There are several ways you can help me get the word out about the message of this book...

- Post a 5-Star review on Amazon.

- Write about the book on your Facebook, Twitter, Instagram – any social media you regularly use!

- If you blog, consider referencing the book, or publishing an excerpt from the book with a link back to my website. You have my permission to do this as long as you provide proper credit and backlinks.

- Recommend the book to friends – word-of-mouth is still the most effective form of advertising.

- Purchase additional copies to give away as gifts. You can do that by going to my website at: www.AndreButler.com

The best way to connect with me is at
www.AndreButler.com

ENJOY THESE OTHER BOOKS
BY ANDRE BUTLER

amazon   BARNES&NOBLE

You can order these books from AMAZON & B&N or where ever you purchase your favorite books. You can also order these books from my website at: www. AndreButler.com

NEED A SPEAKER FOR YOUR
NEXT PROGRAM?

Invite me to speak to your group or ministry. If you would like to have me come speak to your group or at an upcoming event, please contact me at: www.AndreButler.com